THE SWORD

SERVANT OF TRUTH

SERVANT OF TRUTH

CONTENTS

PROLOGUE

*H*ello, brothers and sisters.

I am an ex-addict who spent 33 years in deep, dark addiction. It tiptoed me right to the edge of death—I was living with one foot in the grave. I didn't want to die, but I couldn't seem to stop, even though I knew the drugs and alcohol were killing me. The darkness was real. I could feel it. Sometimes, I even saw it. It was a spiritual darkness trying to consume me.

If you've lived it, you know—there is a spiritual aspect to addiction. The deeper you go, the more obvious it becomes.

I always knew God existed. My mother was a woman of faith. But I never truly tried to know Him. Not until the end. One evening, I was out on my deck at sunset—intoxicated and dying—and I looked up at the beautiful sky and apologized to God. I told Him I was sorry, that I didn't want to die this way, but I couldn't stop. I had made peace with the fact that one day soon, I'd go to sleep and never wake up.

I lived near the hills and prairies of the Midwest, surrounded by wildlife. But that night, something different happened. A little swallow came and hovered in front of me—so close I could've reached out and touched it. It stayed there for over a minute, just cocking its head and looking at me. In that moment, I knew. I knew it was Him. God was letting me know He was there. That He saw me. That He heard me.

That moment changed everything.

Just days later, I went from a downward spiral I couldn't stop to being completely sober—and I have been ever since. God instilled in me a deep love for His Word. Daily reading became my life. I'd been through inpatient and outpatient treatment, counseling, and all kinds of recovery groups. I don't have a degree in addiction counseling—but I've lived it. I've walked through it, surrounded by others just like me. I knew the programs so well by the end that I could tell counselors exactly what they wanted to hear.

But it was faith—only faith—that set me free. That brought true, lasting recovery. I've never once stood in front of a beer cooler or liquor aisle battling the urge to give in. God didn't just help me resist—He removed the desire altogether. When I finally understood that God truly loved me, I was set free.

This program—this book—was given to me by the Holy Spirit. I first used it to start a recovery group at my church. I wrote every word myself. I'm not someone with a master's degree in psychology or addiction science—I'm just a fellow addict, saved by the grace of God.

As I wrote the lessons for our group, I felt led to turn them into a daily devotional for other addicts—something to offer encouragement and structure each day. Then I realized: if I included our group's mission statement, anyone could use this book as either a personal devotional or a guide to start a recovery group of their own. Whether it's just you and a friend, or a whole room full of people, you can adapt this however you need to.

The purpose of this book is simple: to set people free. To give them a peace that surpasses all understanding. Because addiction is a spiritual affliction. And a spiritual affliction requires a spiritual cure.

God's healing is supernatural. When you surrender and let Him heal your spirit, everything else—your mind, your body, your habits—begin to follow.

Using this book for recovery groups:

We start our group by reading the mission statement. When you read it, you'll see the mission of this group is freedom from addiction through Christ. You suffer from addiction, but you are **not defined by it**, and it is not a permanent part of you. When Jesus healed the lame man and he walked, did he still call himself lame? When Jesus healed the blind man and he could see, did he still call himself blind? No. Jesus came to set the captives free.

Next, we do "highs and lows"—the highs and lows from the last week or since the last meeting. Talking about our emotional ups and downs helps build self-awareness. It helps us reflect, with ourselves and the group, on how our emotional state connects to our recovery. It's also just good to share what made you smile—and to release what's weighing you down. Emotional awareness is the goal.

Then we read the devotional entry for the day and answer the reflection questions. Some of these questions may seem simple or rhetorical, but even the simple ones are designed to get us thinking. Sometimes it's the most basic question that opens the door to something deeper we hadn't considered.

When there are more people in the group, this usually fills the whole hour. But I live in a small town and groups are often small. In that case, feel free to go through more than one devotional or keep things flexible. Some groups prefer a deeper focus on one topic. Others prefer more conversation. Go with what works best for your group.

At the end, we ask for any final thoughts, questions, or reflections. Then we do a short accountability share, where we're honest about areas we've struggled. We close in prayer. You can either let everyone pray or designate one person to pray over the group. Again—do what works best for your group.

These groups should be loving and non-judgmental. Confidentiality is **critical**. If people don't feel safe, they won't share, and if they don't share, they won't heal. In my first few months, almost nobody came to group—but I kept going. Maybe your group will be full from day one. Maybe it will just be a few people trying to get free. Maybe it's just two friends showing up consistently. No matter what—**commit**. Make it matter.

I also used different Bible translations depending on the verse—sometimes for clarity, sometimes just because I liked how a version worded it. I personally have a preferred translation, but I believe people should use whichever version of the Bible helps them understand God's Word best.

I can't offer medical advice or psychological diagnoses. What I offer is what God gave me: a man who spent over 30 years in addiction, on the verge of death, who tried every program, group, and treatment imaginable—and was radically set free by the love of God.

I want to share that love with you. I want to see broken people walk in freedom.

There are millions of addicts in this world. And the only thing I'm an expert in is what addiction can do to a life—and how the love of Jesus Christ can set us free.

God bless you. God loves you. I love you. And remember: **you are never alone. Ever.**

MISSION STATEMENT

Blessed Faith Recovery

"*Abraham believed what God told him, and God counted him righteous for it*" *(Genesis 15:6)*

Jesus said, "Your faith has healed you." (Mark 10:52)

God told Isaiah, "If your faith is not firm, I cannot make you stand firm." (Isaiah 7:9)

Faith is the most important aspect of a person's relationship with the Lord. We believe through faith we are not powerless over our addictions, and that through faith we can find freedom from the chains that have held us down, no matter how long they've been there or how strong they feel. Through faith, we can free ourselves, be renewed, and thrive beyond what we thought possible. We can find hope and joy and contentment in our lives, through faith.

We are a faith-based recovery group. We are not adversaries of AA, NA, or any other recovery group. We have a different approach to sobriety and recovery.

We do not believe we are powerless over our addictions, but that through faith in the Lord, we are empowered to overcome our addictions.

We do not identify ourselves as our addictions, but instead as people struggling with addictions.

If addictions are a disease, then there is a cure: we have faith that the cure is Jesus Christ.

Just as in other recovery groups, by attending our group, you have agreed to keep everything at meetings confidential, and everyone attending groups anonymous.

At each meeting:

1. Read introduction

2. Review highs and lows from the week

3. Discuss the Bible verse for the night and how it relates to recovery

4. Other discussion/accountability

5. Prayer requests and closing prayer

CHAPTER ONE

ABBA FATHER

Galatians 4:6 *And because we are His children, God has sent the Spirit of His Son into our hearts, prompting us to call out, "Abba, Father!"*

We are all God's children, and He loves us as such. Abba Father would be the old way of saying Daddy to your dad. It implies that God is close and caring and empathetic to what we go through. Not some far-away deity who doesn't want to be troubled with our problems, but a close and caring parent who lets us make our own choices but is also there to protect and help. He sends the Spirit of His Son into our hearts so that we know this truth—that God loves us more than any person ever could.

Reflection Questions:
- **Does God seem distant to you?**

- **Does this verse make Him more approachable?**

- **Is it hard to understand how the Divine Creator of the universe is also just a loving parent?**

CHAPTER TWO

A NEW PERSPECTIVE

2 Corinthians 6:10 As sorrowful, yet rejoicing; as poor, yet making many rich; as having nothing, yet possessing everything.

The world calls us sorrowful, poor, & having nothing. But we rejoice, make people rich, and have everything we need. There's the way those of the world see the world & then there's the way people who know Jesus Christ see the exact same world. We rejoice in the Lord in all circumstances, we make rich in the knowledge of God & salvation, & have everything we need in this life & the next through our Lord & Savior Jesus Christ. Some see 8 billion people in the world, we see 8 billion children created in the image of the Most High God. Find Jesus & find a new perspective on how good the world is when you know Him.

Reflection Questions:

- **Are you an optimist or a pessimist?**

- **How do you see the world?**

- **How can a relationship with Jesus change your paradigm of the world?**

CHAPTER THREE

A MULTITUDE COVERED

1 Peter 4:7–8 *The end of all things is at hand; therefore be self-controlled and sober-minded for the sake of your prayers. Above all, keep loving one another earnestly, since love covers a multitude of sins.*

"The end of all things" was written over 2000 years ago. But being self-controlled and sober-minded is still a must for all of us for our prayers to find the Lord. Love for each other doesn't even mean certain people — it means having a heart filled with love all the time. Always be kind and treat people well. Addictions may have affected the way we treated the people we love. Don't care about the rest. If our heart posture is love, the Lord is willing to overlook our sins as well.

Reflection Questions:

- **How are self-controlled and sober-minded connected?**

- **How does love cover a multitude of sins?**

- **Why is loving on another earnestly above all?**

CHAPTER FOUR

A BLESSING, NOT A CURSE

Proverbs 18:22 He who finds a wife finds a good thing & obtains favor from the LORD.

He who finds a wife, she who finds a husband finds a good thing. Not a curse but a blessing. Often it is the case that our spouses or significant others take the brunt of the fallout from our addictions. They're in the way of getting our fix, dealing with a hungover & grouchy spouse, telling us what we're doing isn't right, & letting us know the damage it's causing. Things we don't want to hear when we're focused on our fix. Embrace the blessing they are, listen to them. What you take as nagging & complaining can be just them trying to help because they see something wrong.

Reflection Questions:

- **Has your spouse expressed concern about your addiction?**

- **Did you listen?**

- **Could recovery change the nature of your relationships?**

Chapter Five

Able to Help

Hebrews 2:18 For because He Himself has suffered when tempted, He is able to help those who are being tempted.

Jesus Christ—though God—became flesh, and though sinless, faced temptations just as we do. So our God actually empathizes with us in times of temptation. He knows how it feels to be tempted, and is there to be our strength when we are weakest.

Reflection Questions:

- How does it help our recovery to know that Jesus suffered when tempted?

- How is He able to help us?

Chapter Six

ACCEPTABLE WORSHIP

Acceptable Worship Hebrews 12:28 *Therefore let us be grateful for receiving a kingdom that cannot be shaken, and thus let us offer to God acceptable worship, with reverence and awe.*

Being thankful that we are a part of the perfect world to come. The world and everything therein belongs to God, and we are a part of God's family. Reverence and awe for the Creator of the universe who spoke it into existence with a Word, should go without saying. Worship Him with a sober mind, undivided attention, reverence for who He is and awe for all He's done. Worship Him how He wants to be worshipped and not how you've decided is good enough. No one's perfect ever, but God sees a heart that's trying to be the best it can.

Reflection Questions:
- **What are different types of worship?**

- **What is acceptable worship?**

- **Do you worship God in your daily life or just on Sunday?**

CHAPTER SEVEN

BLESSED HOPE

Titus 2:13 Waiting for our blessed hope, the appearing of the glory of our great God and Savior Jesus Christ.

Lack of hope in an addict's life is just the way we exist. Sometimes we've never known hope in any form ever, which is why we struggle with our addictions the way we do. We have no hope, so we numb it with our fix. Temporary, chemically induced happiness to cover the pain of hopelessness. The supernatural hope we are given by Jesus Christ is unlike any other, and once you experience it, you know what true hope is. Hope for a better life, where joy separate from circumstances becomes the way we live.

Reflection Questions:

- **Have you ever had hope?**

- **What kind of things have you hoped for in life?**

- **What kind of hope can our God and Savior Jesus Christ give us?**

Chapter Eight

Appears Right, Ends in Death

Proverbs 14:12 There is a way that appears to be right, but in the end it leads to death.

We can often, as addicts and with an addict mentality, try to convince ourselves just one or two drinks will be OK, or just $10 in the video lottery machine, or just this one time I'll watch porn, then no more. Lying to ourselves in that we can handle just a little of our addiction but won't let it spiral out of control. But it's always just the spark that starts the inferno. That lie leads us to death—sometimes spiritually, but sometimes, depending on what our addiction is, actual death. Don't let indulging your addiction ever appear to be right, because you know the truth of where it leads.

Reflection Questions:
- **What does "a way that appears to be right, but in the**

end leads to death" mean to you and your struggle with
addiction?

CHAPTER NINE

BE HEALED, BE FREE

Mark 5:34 *Daughter, said Jesus, your faith has healed you. Go in peace and be free from your affliction.*

Your faith has healed you or believing that Jesus can heal you is what makes you well. It is what fills the void we try to fill with addictions and worldly things and makes us whole. What a gift to have peace and be free from things that have oppressed us most of our lives. Many of us have spent more of our lives addicted than not, and the part of our lives that led to the addictions mean we've never known freedom or true peace. Have faith, be healed, be free.

Reflection Questions:
- **Where does your faith stand right now?**

- **How can you strengthen it?**

- **Have you ever known true peace?**

Chapter Ten

BE STILL

Psalm 46:10 Be still, and know that I am God.

Sometimes our restless nature as human beings can be one of our worst enemies—to not be content when there's peace in our lives. Or fixing problems by our power and not the Lord's. The Lord makes things the way they should be in His time, and when we've submitted a problem to Him, we trust that He is working on it perfectly. When we pray and submit problems, we can't lose faith or become upset when our problem doesn't immediately get better or disappear. Sometimes they may be solved right away, and sometimes problems that took time to create take time to fix and heal. Trust the process, trust in the Lord Jesus Christ.

Reflection Questions:

• **What does "be still" mean as applied to recovery and to our soul?**

• **Do you have a hard time with stillness?**

• **How do we fight the restlessness inside us?**

Chapter Eleven

BOUGHT AT A PRICE

1 Corinthians 7:2 **You were bought at a price; do not become slaves of men.**

You were bought with the precious blood of our Lord and Savior Jesus Christ in the greatest act of love ever done in this world. A price He paid willingly, because He loves you. Becoming a slave of men means becoming a slave to the things of this world.

In our addictions, our enslavement is voluntary. It was conscious choices we made that led to our bondage. It's also a choice to reach out to the One who sets the captives free, to end that bondage and break those chains. Freedom or slavery, liberty or bondage—the price is already paid. **It's your choice.**

Reflection Questions:

- **Does addiction feel like slavery?**

- **How so, if it does?**

- **Did you know your debt to God was paid for in full?**

CHAPTER TWELVE

CRUCIFIED WITH CHRIST

Galatians 2:20 My old self has been crucified with Christ. It is no longer I who live, but Christ lives in me. So I live in this earthly body by trusting in the Son of God, who loved me and gave His life for me.

Whoever we were, whatever we've done, has been nailed to the cross with Jesus Christ. We are made new, not perfect. Becoming one with Him is a lifelong journey, knowing we'll never be perfect but always we strive to be better. We trust Him with all our hearts, knowing that He loved us enough to die for us.

Reflection Questions:

- **What does it mean "no longer I who live, but Christ lives in me"?**

- **Why does he make it a point to mention living in an earthly body?**

CHAPTER THIRTEEN

COVERED BY GRACE

*P**salm 32:1** Blessed is the one whose transgression is forgiven, whose sin is covered.*

As people, we make our share of mistakes, as addicts we make even more. Addiction makes it easier to override that part of our conscience that says "don't do this, it's wrong." That urge to get our fix wins over the part of us saying—no, I shouldn't do this. The bad news is even in recovery we'll sin and make mistakes. It's a part of the human condition. The good news is when we follow Jesus Christ every transgression, great or small, is forgiven. All our sin is covered. How blessed are we to receive such a gift?

Reflection Questions:

Do you think you've done things God won't forgive?

What sin did His blood not cover?

How do we get this forgiveness?

CHAPTER FOURTEEN

CONFIDENT MERCY

Hebrews 4:16 Therefore let's approach the throne of grace with confidence, so that we may receive mercy and find grace for help at the time of our need.

We shouldn't be ashamed to ask God for help when we are tempted. Sometimes the nature of the thought might make us feel shame that we even had it. Intrusive thoughts, lustful thoughts, thoughts of using, aren't failures in themselves but products of temptations of the enemy or our sinful flesh. When temptation is upon us we confidently ask the Lord for help knowing that He desires to intervene before our thoughts lead to sin.

Reflection Questions:

- **What does approaching the throne of grace with confidence mean?**

- **As addicts, how important is mercy and grace in our time of need?**

- **What is our time of need?**

CHAPTER FIFTEEN

CONFESSION AND FORGIVENESS

P salm 32:5 I acknowledged my sin to you, and I did not cover my iniquity; I said, 'I will confess my transgressions to the LORD,' and you forgave the iniquity of my sin. Selah.

As addicts, not fully acknowledging the mistakes we've made and the people we've hurt can hold us back. It's much easier to say or think, "I wasn't that bad," or "It wasn't that often," or "Everyone is ok now." Instead of saying, "I was not a good person, I wasn't a good parent, I wasn't a good spouse." Being honest about the damage we caused and confessing it to God and asking for forgiveness can let us close that chapter. People may or may not forgive you, but if you ask with a sincere heart, God does every time.

Reflection Questions:
- **Are you honest with yourself about the damage your addiction has caused?**

- **Have you confessed to God and asked forgiveness?**

- **Do you think He'll forgive you?**

Chapter Sixteen

COMPANY THAT CORRUPTS

1 Corinthians 15:33 **Do not be deceived: Bad company corrupts good character.**

Have you ever noticed that even though you may not swear often—or at all—but you start hanging out with someone who swears a lot, you start to swear more?

We know ourselves that addiction doesn't make you a bad person, but you most definitely do things you wouldn't do while sober or not using. So if someone is full-on in addiction, or someone who will try to entice you to use—steer clear.

It's not judging them for doing something you've done yourself, it's doing what's right *for you* and your recovery. If they're offended or don't understand, they may not care about your well-being anyway.

Reflection Questions:

- Do you have a hard time not being around people who

could lead to using?

- How can you tell them as non-judgmentally as possible?

- Where do you find people who can help you stand?

CHAPTER SEVENTEEN

COMMITTED WORK

Proverbs 16:3 Commit your work to the Lord, and your plans will be established.

Commit to the Lord your work toward recovery. Commit to the Lord all the works of your life. If you are attempting to align any work you are doing in life to God's will for your life, He will help you establish that work. Don't think what you are trying to do—think what does He want me to do. Working by our own power is futile and has been proven futile in all of our lives, but seeking His will for our lives taps us into His divine power helping us to succeed.

Reflection Questions:

• **What are some of the works in your life you'd like to commit to the Lord?**

• **How do you do that?**

CHAPTER EIGHTEEN

CLING TO THE WORD

Psalm 68:11 *The Lord gave the Word; great was the company of those who proclaimed it.*

The Lord gave us His Word to know Him, to learn about Him, about the people who came before us, how we're supposed to live, about His glory, His grace, His love. The hope and inner peace we long for lies within it. Great was the company who proclaimed it, and they were all imperfect people like us, but in all their imperfections they clung to His Word.

Reflection Questions

- **Do you make time for the Word?**

- **How much of a priority is it to you?**

- **What fills your time that is more important?**

CHAPTER NINETEEN

CLEANSED BY THE BLOOD

Hebrews 9:14 *How much more will the blood of Christ, who through the eternal Spirit offered Himself without blemish to God, purify our conscience from dead works to serve the Living God.*

The blood of Christ washes clean all sinners. As addicts our sins are many, the weight of the guilt of these sins can be a burden to the progress we are trying to make in recovery. Sometimes the guilt is so heavy the emotions that follow can lead to relapse. But Christ's unblemished, perfect sacrifice washed us clean & we must allow it to do its work & not hold onto sins that have been forgiven. Those works are dead, let your conscience be purified. Serve the Living God who loves you.

Reflection Questions:

- **Is your guilt still a hurdle to your recovery?**

- **If God has forgiven you shouldn't you let that guilt go?**

- **Was Christ's sacrifice sufficient to cover even your worst sins?**

Chapter Twenty

CHASING THE WIND

E cclesiastes 5:10 **He who loves money will not be satisfied with money, nor he who loves wealth with his income; this also is vanity.**

Chasing worldly things is a self-perpetuating cycle that never ends. Whether it's money, drugs, alcohol, sex, gambling, etc... it's a desire that can never be sated, a hole that can never be filled, only producing a desire for more. Chase the Lord & watch the power worldly desires have over you disintegrate. Chase the Lord & see your spirit filled with peace & contentment. Chase the Lord & watch that emptiness inside you, you tried vainly to fill with worldly things, be full & your heart be made whole again.

Reflection Questions:
- **Do you chase worldly things now?**

- **How do you feel when you occasionally attain what you're chasing?**

- **Does it last or is it temporary?**

CHAPTER TWENTY-ONE

CHOOSE YOUR COMPANY

Proverbs 13:20 **Whoever walks with the wise becomes wise, but the companion of fools suffers harm.**

Plain and simple—who you hang out with matters. Recovery becomes that much harder, if not impossible, if you're hanging out with people who are indulging in things you're trying to be set free from. Just being around them can present its own temptations, but they often also offer us the poison that's destroying us. Be very careful of the company you keep while in recovery.

Reflection Questions:

- **What changes might you have to make with your social circles in order for your recovery to succeed?**

- **How do you do this in a loving way that tries not to hurt people you care about?**

CHAPTER TWENTY-TWO

CAST YOUR BURDEN

P salm 55:22 Cast your burden on the LORD, and He will sustain you; He will never permit the righteous to be moved.

The burdens of life itself can feel crushing sometimes. Throw some of the dysfunction of addiction on top, and it's more than we can bear. These things we use to numb the burden or temporarily distract from the pressures only compound problems and multiply the problems and pressures we deal with. Ask the Lord to help bear your burden. Wisdom and levelheadedness are invaluable when the pressures of life mount. Inner peace over temporary distraction builds a support system within yourself that leads to wise decisions and clear-headed problem solving. He will sustain you and hold you firm when the storms of life buffet you.

Reflection Questions:
- **Are your burdens overwhelming?**

- **How do we cast our burden on the LORD?**

- **How does He sustain us?**

Chapter Twenty-Three

CAST IT ALL

1 Peter 5:6–7 *Humble yourselves, therefore, under the mighty hand of God so that at the proper time He may exalt you, casting all your anxieties on Him because He cares for you.*

Humble yourself — tell Him, Lord, I cannot stop this thing that's hurting me, my loved ones, my health.... All of those worries you have that cause you to fall, cast on Him. He asks you to, and takes them on willingly. He cares for you. He created you. "I got this" won't get it done. God's got this He, gets it done every time. The mighty hand of God will act on your behalf. There is no greater comfort... period.

Reflection Questions

- **Is it a sign of weakness admitting you can't handle something?**

- **What are the ways casting your anxieties on Him could work?**

- **Does God always care for us, or just when we're good and doing well and not indulging our addiction?**

Chapter Twenty-Four

CALL ON THE NAME

Acts 2:21 And it shall come to pass that everyone who calls upon the name of the Lord shall be saved.

There is no one too far gone or who has committed too many sins that they cannot call on the name of the Lord and be saved. No matter how dirty and sinful and unworthy you feel, call on His name and be saved! Do not elevate your sin above the blood of our Savior because there is no sin above it to those who call on Him.

Reflection Questions:
- **What makes people hesitant to call on the name of the Lord?**
- **What does calling on the name of the Lord mean exactly?**

Chapter Twenty-Five
CALL ON HIM

Psalm 138:3 On the day I called, you answered me; my strength of soul you increased.

We can call on the Lord, any day, any time, for any reason. He is our strength, but we must call on Him. He's waiting to help, but we must call on Him. Sometimes we'll sit in our own thoughts, feelings, anger, bitterness, depression, or anxiety and let them be the result. Such a simple step that many believers still do not do in times of temptation and weakness—call on Him, and He will strengthen your soul.

Reflection Questions:
- **How do we call Him?**

- **Why is strength of soul important for recovery?**

- **Why do we hesitate to call on Him?**

CHAPTER TWENTY-SIX

DIVINE INTERVENTION

Psalm 9:10 And those who know Your name put their trust in You, for You, O Lord, have not forsaken those who seek You.

Those who know His name know that He is the Creator of all things, the Most High God, and if we have even a small understanding of who He is, how can we not trust Him? He tells us to call on Him. He who measures the heavens with His hand hears you when you ask Him for help. Not only does He not forsake us when we ask Him for help, He intervenes. Trust Him, seek Him—because God knows we could all use a little divine intervention.

Reflection Questions:

- **Do you know who God is?**

- **How do you learn about Him?**

- **What has made you hesitate to seek Him?**

- **Do we have to be living right before we do?**

CHAPTER TWENTY-SEVEN

DON'T BE TROUBLED

John 14:1 Don't let your hearts be troubled. Believe in God; believe also in Me.

Letting our worries in everyday life overwhelm our thoughts and emotions will lead to relapse if we let it. When Jesus is saying "believe," He is saying: trust God, trust Me. When that burden is heavy and your mind is consumed, pray for relief, open your Bible. Churning minds can't focus on solutions.

Reflection Questions:

- **What kinds of things in life trouble our hearts?**

- **What actions do we take to put our trust in Jesus?**

- **Why can we trust Him with everyday problems?**

Chapter Twenty-Eight

DISCIPLINED NOT DISQUALIFIED

1 Corinthians **9:27 But I discipline my body and keep it under control, lest after preaching to others I myself should become disqualified.**

The physical part of addiction can be a problem in itself. Sometimes even if we have some recovery under our belt, something we saw or smelled or tasted can still spark a physical urge in us for our fix.

A desire. A thought that—*maybe just one more time it would be nice...*

Grace pulls us out of the darkness and is always key, but discipline is how we maintain our recovery without stumbling. Because a stumble can lead to a fall—and a fall to being disqualified.

Reflections Questions:

- **How much self-discipline do you have?**

- **Have you been completely out of control before?**

- **How do we implement discipline in our lives?**

CHAPTER TWENTY-NINE

DEMOLISH STRONGHOLDS

2 Corinthians 10:4–5 The weapons we fight with are not the weapons of this world. On the contrary, they have divine power to demolish strongholds. We demolish arguments and every pretension that sets itself up against the knowledge of God, and we take every thought captive to make it obedient to Christ.

We wield prayer and time in the Word (which is the sword of the Spirit) to conquer the very things that have held us in bondage. We don't hope fleetingly that we might overcome our addictions, **we DEMOLISH STRONGHOLDS!** We take our tempting thoughts captive to bring our mind, body, and spirit into obedience and submission to Jesus Christ our Lord, who loves us and wants us to be free.

Reflection Questions:
- **What are our weapons and how do we wield them?**

- **Why is demolishing arguments and pretensions impor-**

tant?

- **How do we take thoughts captive?**

CHAPTER THIRTY

DELIGHT IN THE WORD

Jeremiah 15:16 *Your words were found, and I ate them, and your words became to me a great joy and the delight of my heart, for I am called by your name, O LORD, God of hosts.*

Connecting with the Word is the foundation of your personal relationship with God. It's how we know Him. It's how we know how He wants us to act, to interact with Him and each other. Start small and work your way up if you struggle. Make time with an open mind and an open heart, and His words will become a great joy to you. Revelations in the Word can give you chills and make your whole day. Let Him delight your heart through His Word. Learn wisdom and knowledge not of this world.

Reflection Questions

- **Do you make time to read the Word?**

- **How does it become a priority rather than a "when I have time"?**

- **Where in your life could you take time from the world to make time for God?**

CHAPTER THIRTY-ONE
DEEP WATERS

P salm 18:16 *He reached down from heaven and rescued me; He drew me out of deep waters.*

Deep waters—something addicts are very familiar with. Addiction gets us in over our heads often. Money spent, loved ones hurt, in trouble at work—the list goes on and on. Sometimes we can't save ourselves. Sometimes we've never even tried. When we're drowning in deep waters we got ourselves into, the Lord will reach down and rescue us. Even when it's our own fault, His love for us doesn't want to see us drown. So do what any drowning person does—call for help.

Reflection Questions:

- **How has your addiction made deep waters for you?**

- **Do you feel like you're drowning sometimes?**

- **Have you called out for help?**

Chapter Thirty-Two

DAYS OF LIGHT

1 John 2:8 *At the same time, it is a new commandment that I am writing to you, which is true in Him and true in you, because the darkness is passing away and the true light is already shining.*

To love one another, that is the commandment. To have a heart of love. As addicts we know we have had hearts of depression, resentment, anger, self-loathing—the list goes on. Hearts of love don't just affect the way you treat those you love. Operating with a loving heart makes everyday life easier. The world ceases to be such a cold, uncaring place for you. You can brighten someone's day by just smiling and saying hi. The darkness is already passing away, so leave it behind and let the true light of Jesus Christ shine through you.

Reflection Questions:

- **Does your current heart have more light days or dark days?**

- **How do you move to have more days of light?**

- **How do light or dark days affect your recovery?**

CHAPTER THIRTY-THREE

ETERNAL WEIGHT

2 Corinthians 4:17–18 For this light momentary affliction is preparing us an eternal weight of glory beyond all comparison, as we look not to the things that are seen but to the things that are unseen. For the things that are seen are transient, but the things that are unseen are eternal.

Our addiction can feel like a life sentence. It's been there so long and done so much damage—but it is momentary. Fix your attention on the Spirit that brings freedom instead of the worries and troubles before you which lead to a need for escape or numbness. Our circumstances are always moving, but your faith in the Lord never should.

Reflection Questions:

- **How do we focus on Jesus Christ above the world right in front of us?**

- **Can that eternal weight of glory beyond all comparison be experienced in this life? How?**

CHAPTER THIRTY-FOUR

ETERNAL WORD

L **uke 21:33 Heaven and earth will pass away, but My words will not pass away.**

The words of Jesus will be here forever, even after the world and universe as we know it no longer exist. What words do we hang our certainty of Christ's help in? "I will never leave you. I will neve r forsake you. No one can snatch you from My hand. Just as the Father has loved Me, I have also loved you; abide in love. Come to Me, all who are weary and burdened, and I will give you rest." Stand on the eternal, unfailing words of Jesus Christ who loves you. Read them and get to know them — freedom lies within them.

Reflection Questions:

- **Have you ever read your Bible consistently?**

- **Do you know how much God loves you?**

- **Have you experienced unconditional love before?**

- **How could unconditional love change who you are?**

Chapter Thirty-Five

EYES FORWARD

P *roverbs 4:25 Let your eyes look directly forward, and your gaze be straight before you.*

The best way to keep from stumbling and falling is by keeping your eyes on the path, not by looking back at where you've already walked. Wherever you've been and whatever you've done God doesn't care about your past as long as you're trusting in Him now. To repent is to change your mind, to turn away. Repentance doesn't equal perfection but it's a mind and a heart that no longer embrace the things we used to but embrace the Lord instead. Look ahead to who you are becoming and not back to who you were.

Reflection Questions:

- **Does your past hinder your progress sometimes?**

- **Do you find letting go hard or does it excite you?**

- **How does God help us be focused forward and before us?**

CHAPTER THIRTY-SIX

EYES OPENED

Acts 26:18 *to open their eyes so that they may turn from darkness to light and from the power of Satan to God, that they may receive forgiveness of sins and a place among those who are sanctified by faith in Me.*

Those are Jesus' words. To open our eyes and see that where we are in addiction and the way we live are wrong. You would think that turning away from something that causes so much pain and destruction would be easy—a no-brainer. But that is not the nature of addiction. Once our eyes are open—even if it happens while we're still bound—it's on us to turn from darkness to light. There's miraculous news: Jesus Christ is there to help. To forgive you, to sanctify you, and to show you the joy of living in the light.

Reflection Questions:

- **Do you notice the battle between Satan and God within your addiction?**

- **Are your eyes truly open to the realities of both sides?**

CHAPTER THIRTY-SEVEN

FAITH THAT HEALS

Mark 10:52 And Jesus said to him, "Go your way; your faith has made you well." And immediately he recovered his sight & followed Him on the way.

Healed not because he tried really hard or did anything of his own power, but because he had faith. Your faith that Jesus can do what you can't or couldn't is what heals you. Don't look for the strength inside yourself to overcome your addiction, submit to your faith in Jesus Christ & He will heal you. Once you find that faith lean into it with all your heart & do exactly what this man did—follow Him on the way.

Reflection Questions:
- **Where does your faith stand right now?**

- **Do you believe Jesus can heal you?**

- **Why or why not?**

CHAPTER THIRTY-EIGHT

FAITHFUL IN CHAINS

*G*enesis 39:21 But the LORD was with Joseph in the prison and showed him his faithful love. And the LORD made Joseph a favorite with the prison warden.

Even when the worst of the worst of circumstances are upon us God is with us using those circumstances to our benefit if we only trust in Him. Joseph's circumstances and imprisonment were not of his doing as addicts ours usually are. Even through imprisonment where he had committed no crime, Joseph kept his faith. We often imprison ourselves and blame God. When you're in the worst of times, stand firm. Keep the faith. If you curse God when things are bad He may leave you to the whims of the world. If you stand firm in your faith He'll use those to your benefit and you'll be a better person when they're over.

Reflection Questions:
- **What are some of the worst things you've faced due to addiction?**

- **Is God willing to help even in self-inflicted situations?**

- **Why was God with Joseph?**

CHAPTER THIRTY-NINE

FAITHFUL PROMISE

Hebrews 10:23 Let us hold fast to the confession of our hope without wavering, for He who promised is faithful.

To hold fast to the confession of our hope in Jesus Christ our Lord and Savior. So easy to hit some bad circumstances and start to lose hope, doubt our faith or our worthiness to receive help. This verse tells us no matter what things look like or what we do or how things seem or how we feel, but instead to stand firm in what we KNOW. We know the He is faithful. He keeps every promise He makes, and He never, ever leaves us. Don't let your circumstances make you uncertain, stand on the certainty of who Jesus is.

Reflection Questions:

- **Do you feel like your faith is strong or not strong?**

- **Have you thought it was strong, but had it shaken before?**

- **Do you believe Jesus Christ is faithful?**

- **How do we build spiritual strength?**

CHAPTER FORTY

FAITHFUL TO FORGIVE

1 **John 1:9 If we confess our sins, He is faithful & just to forgive us our sins and to cleanse us from all unrighteousness.**

Confession in itself is a burden lifted. Old skeletons, things we've done because of our addictions can be an everyday mental weight we carry. But God is faithful, always faithful even through the worst of our worst. He forgives us if we confess our sins to Him. And cleanses us from the unrighteousness our choices have brought upon us. The blood of Christ has washed us clean. Yes, God knows every sin we have committed anyway, but confession shows submission to Him and His judgment and lets Him forgive and cleanse us to start over and live a good life.

Reflection Questions:

- **Have you ever confessed to God?**

- **How would we go about doing that?**

- **What is Godly forgiveness & cleansing?**

CHAPTER FORTY-ONE

FAVOR FROM THE LORD

Proverbs 18:22 **He who finds a wife finds a good thing and obtains favor from the LORD.**

He who finds a wife, she who finds a husband finds a good thing. Not a curse but a blessing. Often it is the case that our spouses or significant others take the brunt of the fallout from our addictions. They're in the way of getting our fix, dealing with a hungover and grouchy spouse, telling us what we're doing isn't right, and letting us know the damage it's causing. Things we don't want to hear when we're focused on our fix. Embrace the blessing they are, listen to them. What you take as nagging and complaining can be just them trying to help because they see something wrong.

Reflection Questions:

- **Has your spouse expressed concern about your addiction?**

- **Did you listen?**

- **Could recovery change the nature of your relationship?**

Chapter Forty-Two

FEAR THE LORD

Fear the Lord **Proverbs 23:17 Let not your heart envy sinners, but continue to fear the LORD all the day.**

Those old urges and temptations, when we see people who indulge their sin freely, can put us in a bind. Remembering the good times and the pleasure can be easy, but if you feel this coming on, make sure to remind yourself of the damage it did and the pain it caused. It isn't where we want to dwell, but it is where we want to go when we find ourselves envying people laughing and having fun doing what we used to do. Fear the LORD means we care about what He thinks above any other, including yourself.

Reflection Questions:

- **Do you see people still indulging in vices, and it makes you wish, even for a moment?**

- **How can you stop that feeling?**

- **Does what the Lord thinks matter to you? How much?**

Chapter Forty-Three

Filled Life

John 7:37 On the last day of the feast, the great day, Jesus stood up and cried out, If anyone thirsts, let them come to me and drink.

No, Jesus wasn't talking about a cold glass of water during a rough hangover! He was talking about living water. Spiritual water for thirsty souls. Hope for the hopeless. Life for the dead inside. Spiritual rejuvenation to people trying to fill a hole inside them with things of this world, to no avail. He wasn't offering a drink of water. He was offering a new joy and hope-filled life.

Reflection Questions:

- Have you ever felt like your life's ever had true meaning?

- Have you ever felt like there was something missing inside you?

- Have you ever given Jesus a true chance to change your life?

Chapter Forty-Four

FIX YOUR GAZE ON THE LORD

Psalm 16:8 I have set the LORD always before me; because He is at my right hand, I will not be shaken.

We keep our eyes fixed on the LORD through any & every circumstance. Prison, jail, in the doghouse, facing the repercussions our addictions have brought on us. When you keep your focus on the Lord, prison is no longer prison & we can face the world with the assurance that He is with us, beside us, upholding us and giving us hope where there is none. There's not a man in the Bible that never faced adversity, even Jesus. But those that set the Lord before them endured it & thrived. Replace fear, anger, anxiety, & depression with hope & strength. Fix your gaze on the Lord and become unshakeable.

Reflection Questions:

- **Is it hard to focus on the Lord because of our circumstances sometimes?**

- **How do we strengthen that focus?**

- **Are there problems & situations that are too big for Him?**

CHAPTER FORTY-FIVE

FRUIT OF REPENTANCE

Luke 3:8 Bear fruit in keeping with repentance. And do not begin to say to yourselves, We have Abraham as our father. For I tell you, God is able to raise from these stones children for Abraham.

Or as the NLT says—Prove by the way you live that you have repented of your sins and turned to God. Don't let the fact that because through Christ we are made children of Abraham let you make sin tolerable because you are forgiven. Stand firm in the new creation you have become.

Reflection Questions:

- How do we walk the line between allowing ourselves to be human and make mistakes, and not letting ourselves be tolerant of sin in our lives?

- What does "God is able to raise up children of Abraham from these stones" mean to us?

Chapter Forty-Six

GRACE TO WORK IT OUT

1 Corinthians 15:10 *But by the grace of God I am what I am, and His grace toward me was not in vain. On the contrary, I worked harder than any of them—though it was not I, but the grace of God that is with me.*

Thank God that you are what you are—His child, created in His image. Don't let things you've done define who you are. Recovery is hard work, but well worth it. So do the work, don't cut corners, stop procrastinating on necessary changes. You will be working hard, but the grace of God will be right with you, helping you get it done.

Reflection Questions

- **Do you take your recovery seriously?**

- **Is hard work intimidating to you?**

- **Do you feel like by the grace of God you are who you are?**

- **How does the grace help you with the work?**

CHAPTER FORTY-SEVEN

GRACE AND ADDICTION

L uke 15:7 I tell you, in the same way there will be more rejoicing in heaven over one sinner who repents than over 99 righteous persons who do not need to repent.

When you change your path and turn to the Lord, heaven rejoices. No matter the number or severity, heaven celebrates the lost sheep returned home. Don't let your own self-condemnation keep you from turning to God. We deem ourselves unworthy. He does not. We are His lost children, and our Father waits for us to return. Getting lost is easy for us flawed people; if we turn to the Lord, so is finding our way home.

Reflection Questions:

- **Have you or do you feel lost?**

- **What could make the Lord not accept you if you re- pented and turned to Him?**

- **Who rejoices if you change your ways and return to**

God?

Chapter Forty-Eight

GODLINESS WITH CONTENTMENT

1 Timothy 6:6–7 But godliness with contentment is great gain. For we brought nothing into the world and we cannot take anything out of the world.

As addicts, restlessness and discontent become just the way we exist. Always looking to our next fix or next party or whatever it is we think we want to do. Godliness with contentment brings an ability to be where we are in the moment and at peace. That mind that can't stop running over scenarios that haven't happened and aren't going to is turned off. Connection with the Most High God is why we exist, so when we find it, contentment comes naturally. We brought nothing in and can take nothing out — so find the One who can give you joy in this life and the next.

Reflection Questions:

- **Do you struggle to be content?**

- **What does godliness with contentment mean to you?**

- **How could it change your everyday life?**

Chapter Forty-Nine

GOD'S CHOSEN ONES

Colossians 3:12 *Put on then, as God's chosen ones, holy and beloved, compassionate hearts, kindness, humility, meekness, and patience.*

If you're wondering, yes — if you're here now reading this, you are God's chosen. Only His Spirit can call you to seek Him. Holy, because Jesus Christ paid for every mistake you've made with His blood, and that's how God sees you. Why? Because you are beloved by Him. Showing other people all the loving traits here heals you as well. When we engage bitterness, anger, judgment, etc., it emanates to our spirit and steals our peace. Walk in love and watch the very essence of who you are change.

Reflection Questions
- **Do you feel like God's chosen one?**

- **What should we align ourselves with — how we see ourselves, or how God sees us?**

- **How can treating others lovingly bring you peace?**

CHAPTER FIFTY

GOD BREATHED

J **ob 32:8 But it is the spirit in man, the breath of the Almighty, that makes him understand.**

God has breathed our spirit and intelligence into us, it is a piece of Him inside of us. It is the part of us that is our consciousness, our understanding and intellect. We have a light inside of us which we try to power with batteries of this world. As addicts, these batteries are our vices, a temporary boost for a flicker of light which dims quickly and becomes so dim that we can't feel any shine. So we throw away the batteries and plug directly into the source. That piece of God in us doesn't make us God, but when we plug that piece of God into Him from whom it came, its light shines brightly and constantly. So plug into the source and never need batteries again.

Reflection Questions:

- **Did you know that your spirit was God breathed?**

- **What else does the Bible say is God breathed?**

- **Do you think there's a connection?**

CHAPTER FIFTY-ONE

GLORY AND DOMINION

Jude 25 **To the only God, our Savior, through Jesus Christ our Lord, be glory, majesty, dominion, and authority, before all time and now and forever. Amen.**

When we've tried everything we can think of, tried everything in our power but are still bound, still suffering, still damaging our lives and relationships — where can we turn? To the only God and Savior, Jesus Christ our Lord. All of that glory, majesty, dominion, and authority is there waiting for us to call on Him, wanting us to call on Him. Freedom is just a heartfelt prayer away. Sometimes it's instantaneous and sometimes it's a process — everyone's journey with Him is different. Infinite, eternal power waiting to show you how much He loves you.

Reflection Questions:
- **Who is Jesus Christ to you?**

- **Do you believe He can set you free?**

- **If yes, why?**

- **If no, why?**

Chapter Fifty-Two

GIFT OF GOD

Ephesians 2:8 For by grace you have been saved through faith. And this is not your own doing; it is the gift of God.

When we believe in and lean on God, we receive His grace. We are encouraged because being not of our own doing means we don't have to accomplish it by our good deeds or righteousness but by our faith that He is our God. He loves us; He wants us to be free.

Reflection Questions:

- **What does God's grace entail to an addict?**

- **How can we actively strengthen our faith?**

- **What does being saved mean to you?**

Chapter Fifty-Three

GET BACK UP

Proverbs 24:16 For the righteous falls seven times and rises again, but the wicked stumble in times of calamity.

No matter how many slips, stumbles, backslides or relapses happen during your recovery, get up and start marching toward recovery again! You only fail if you stop trying. Divine forgiveness is immeasurable, and the Lord will never stop helping you — even think a wicked heart doesn't care. A wicked heart doesn't care about recovery, only indulgence. If you're pursuing recovery, your heart is pointed in the right direction. Never stop getting up — we all fall short.

Reflection Questions:

- **Have you fallen before while seeking recovery?**

- **Does it make you feel hopeless?**

- **Is it hopeless?**

CHAPTER FIFTY-FOUR

HOLD FAST

Hebrews 10:23 Let us hold fast the confession of our hope without wavering, for He who promised is faithful.

The confession of our hope. Our hope is that Jesus Christ can help us be better than we've ever been & do things we never thought possible. Hold fast. Don't lose faith every time trials or struggles are in your life. If you lose faith every time there's a hardship, it's not really faith at all. He who promised never promised perpetual calm seas, He did promise to be next to us through the storm.

Reflection Questions:

- **What does "hold fast" mean in this verse?**

- **Do you believe God is faithful?**

- **Have you ever given Him a chance to be?**

CHAPTER FIFTY-FIVE

HIS FRIEND

Psalm 25:14 The friendship of the LORD is for those who fear Him, and He makes known to them His covenant.

The LORD is not an inaccessible far-off God. To fear Him means only to be in awe of Him—His power, His greatness—but also for us, His grace, mercy, and love. Be in awe of Him and be His friend. Learn from Him things that you never thought you'd know. Knowing Him is true freedom and where hope that never dies lies.

Reflection Questions:

- **Have you ever considered friendship with God as a possibility?**

- **How does He make known to you His covenant?**

CHAPTER FIFTY-SIX

HELP FROM THE LORD

Psalm 121:1–2 I lift my eyes up to the hills. From where does my help come? My help comes from the LORD, who made heaven and earth.

When we're knocked down, beat up, tried time and time again to get our lives together and failed — our help comes from the Creator of all things. What greater help could we ask for than the God that knew us before He knit us together in our mother's womb. There is none greater. There is none more willing to forgive all we've done. The better we know Him, the easier this is to wrap our minds around. So start getting to know Him, start today.

Reflection Questions:

- **Have you ever felt like a helpless observer in your own life?**

- **How alone have you felt?**

- **Are we ever alone and helpless if we embrace the Lord?**

Chapter Fifty-Seven

Healing the Outcast

Jeremiah 30:17 For I will restore health to you, and your wounds I will heal, declares the Lord, because they have called you an outcast: It is Zion, for whom no one cares!

In the life of addiction, sometimes we become outcasts—but of our own making. Outcast from society, family, friends, children, and spouses. But God seeks the outcasts for restoration, the underdogs for victory. We must let Him restore our health and heal our wounds—whether relationships, emotional, mental, or physical—but spiritual healing is the key to all other wounds being healed. Let the Lord heal your spirit so that all other wounds may be healed.

Reflection Questions:
- **How has your addiction made you an outcast?**

- **Why is spiritual healing the cornerstone for all healing?**

Chapter Fifty-Eight

Healer of Faithlessness

Jeremiah 3:22 Return, O faithless children, and I will heal your faithlessness. Here we are; we come to you, for You are the Lord our God.

Through constant disobedience and falling away, God never turned His back on His children. Angry but patient and loving, always forgiving beyond what they deserve. There's no such thing as too many times for God to forgive. We go to Him because He is the Lord our God who loves and cares about us.

Reflection Questions:

- **How have you been faithless in your life?**

- **What does the Lord mean by "heal you of your faithlessness"?**

Chapter Fifty-Nine

Healed and Whole Again

Revelation 22:2 *Through the middle of the city; also, on either side of the river grew a tree of life with its 12 kinds of fruit, yielding its fruit each month. The leaves of the tree were for healing the nations.*

The river of life, from He who promised us living waters, that if we drank would never thirst again. A life of addiction can leave us beat up and beat down. Hurting inside and out. Hurt spirits, hurt minds, hurt bodies—hopeless and helpless. Let Jesus Christ, who can heal the nations, mend your wounds. Let the Great Physician make you healthy and whole again.

Reflection Questions

- Are you in need of healing?

- What kinds of wounds has addiction inflicted on you?

- How do we get Jesus to heal us?

CHAPTER SIXTY

HE WILL HELP

Isaiah 40:31 But they who wait for the LORD shall renew their strength; they will soar high on wings like eagles. They will run and not grow weary. They will walk and not faint.

We can feel beat down, hopeless, and in despair when addiction has its hold on us. Like this thing I hate is killing me but I just can't stop. Even in the depths call out to Him and have your strength renewed. To soar, to be free. While running life's race, find power beyond yourself. To walk the narrow path and not grow faint. Wait for Him, call on Him and He will help. He does hear you, He does care, He does love you.

Reflection Questions:
- **What does it mean to wait for the LORD?**
- **Why would He have you wait?**
- **What does spiritual renewal mean?**

CHAPTER SIXTY-ONE

HE MUST INCREASE

John 3:30 He must increase, but I must decrease.

We increase the influence of God in us by making an intentional effort to do godly things. We read our Bible consistently, we pray throughout the day, we go to Bible study, church, etc... Fill yourself with Him and those things, and the world's influence will wane. When we decrease ourselves so that the Spirit of the Lord can come in, the influence and the change in the quality of our life is revolutionary. We become better than we ever thought we could be. Anger, restlessness, depression, and anxiety are no longer forces affecting our lives. Instead, peace, patience, kindness, even temperateness is our default. Increasing Him and decreasing doesn't mean you not being you; it means you being a better, sober you.

Reflection Questions:

- **How have you tried to increase Him in your life?**

- **How can you do so?**

- **If I decrease me, am I still me?**

Chapter Sixty-Two

He Heals the Brokenhearted

Psalm 147:3 He heals the brokenhearted and binds up their wounds.

We in recovery know what a broken heart and being wounded feels like. The broken heartedness and wounds we suffered that helped lead to our addiction; the broken heartedness and wounds we suffered as a result of our addictions; and the broken heartedness and wounds we've inflicted on others as a result of our addictions. We must give the Great Physician the dedication and time to heal us. A lifetime of wounds and broken heartedness won't always be fixed instantaneously, but over time. So that we learn to seek Him, to know Him, and to trust Him.

Reflection Questions:

- **Why does the Lord heal us and bind up our wounds?**

- **Does your heart feel broken?**

- **How do we move on from these things?**

Chapter Sixty-Three

INTEGRITY IN HIS PRESENCE

Psalm 41:12 **But You have upheld me because of my integrity and set me in Your presence forever.**

Integrity is honesty and a refusal to compromise what you know is right. It means you are morally principled and have a sense of uprightness. No one is perfect, ever. But making a sincere effort to be a moral, upright person goes a long way in recovery.

Lies and a "do what you want" attitude are trademarks of addiction and separate you from the Father. He sees when you're genuinely trying and keeps you in His presence—and when that's where you are, recovery is no longer just your fight.

Reflection Questions:

- **Is it hard to be honest with yourself?**

- **When you've been in addiction, how compromised has your integrity become?**

- **Have you been in God's presence before?**

Chapter Sixty-Four

IMAGE OF GOD

Genesis 1:26 Then God said, Let Us make man in Our image, to be like Us. They will reign over the fish in the sea, the birds in the sky, the livestock, all the wild animals on the earth, and the small animals that scurry on the ground.

As we were created in the image of the living God, we were intended to have dominion over all the earth. Yet as addicts, we have ceded dominion over our own lives. We can reclaim that authority through the last Adam, Jesus Christ. When we let a worldly addiction rule us, we are its servant. When we break those chains through Christ, the Prince of Peace, a peace that surpasses all understanding will follow.

Reflection Questions:

- **What does being made in the image of God mean?**

- **What elements of our addiction do we seek to reign over?**

- **Who is "us"?** *(See also: Revelation 19:13, John 1:1–5)*

Chapter Sixty-Five

JOY IN THE WORD

Jeremiah 15:16 Your words were found, and I ate them, and your words became to me a joy and the delight of my heart, for I am called by your name, O Lord, God of hosts.

If getting sober or recovery is your goal, and connection with the Lord is the way, then through His Word is how you get there. Being too busy or not having time is no excuse. Get to know Him through His Word. Sacrificing some TV or phone time to know His Word is not only possible—it may be the most beneficial move you can make towards recovery, and the rewards are beyond measure.

Reflection Questions:

- **What activities in your life could you do less of to make time for the Word?**

- **What do those activities contribute to your life?**

- **Do they sometimes actually hinder recovery or cause temptation?**

Chapter Sixty-Six

JOY IN TRIALS

James 1:2–4 Count it all joy, my brothers, when you meet trials of various kinds, for you know that the testing of your faith produces perseverance. And let perseverance have its full effect, that you may be perfect & complete, lacking in nothing.

Embrace adversity in life. It's the trials that make us strong, build our character, and teach us to lean on the Lord all the time. Every trial we make it through builds our faith and building our faith strengthens our perseverance. As addicts we look to those trials as an excuse to fall and use. How much better are we when through the Lord, we find a way to stand and eventually refuse to fall. When the Lord is our Rock we find joy even in the trials of life.

Reflection Questions:
- **Have you ever thought adversity could be joy?**

- **Have you used trials as an excuse to use?**

- **Are you ready to stand up and persevere?**

CHAPTER SIXTY-SEVEN

JUDGED BY ONE

1 Corinthians 4:3 **But with me it is a very small thing that I should be judged by you or any human court. In fact, I do not even judge myself.**

Don't worry about what other people think about you. Some people will never stop identifying you by the mistakes you've made—it's just the way the world works. But you are no longer of the world, so those opinions should be a very small thing to you. Do not even judge yourself, for there is one Judge, and one Judge alone—God.

Correct yourself if you do something wrong, but ask God for forgiveness and leave the judging to Him. It might sound crazy, but He is much more patient and forgiving than mankind is. He's always merciful, always patient, always loving.

Reflection Questions:
- **Does the perceived judgment of others get to you sometimes?**

- Is there freedom in only accepting God as judge?

- Does not judging yourself mean do whatever you want?

Chapter Sixty-Eight

JUDGE YOURSELF TRULY

1 Corinthians 11:31 **But if we judged ourselves truly, we would not be judged.**

If we judge ourselves truly—or if we are honest with ourselves—facing the reality of the bleakness or hopelessness of the state of our being can be very hard. To look inside yourself and face with honesty the pain you've caused, the damage you've done, is painful but necessary.

It not only keeps the Lord from having to step in and give you a reality check, it lets you fully say: *That's not who I want to be anymore.*

Reflection Questions:

- **Is it hard to take accountability for some of the things you've done in addiction?**

- **Is it better to be too hard or too soft on yourself?**

- **Why is judging yourself a key to freedom from addiction and forging a relationship with God?**

CHAPTER SIXTY-NINE

LET IT GO

E phesians 4:31 Let all bitterness and wrath and anger and clamor and slander be put away from you, along with all malice.

In order to heal and find peace from the things that have led us into addiction, we must forgive wholeheartedly and embrace the path ahead. We cannot move forward while we cling to things behind us. Every negative emotion in this verse can hinder recovery and healing. Forgiveness is crucial for progress toward Christ Jesus and freedom through Him. We do not forgive to make our offenders feel better, but to free our own minds and spirits from the time and energy we spend on them and to walk in obedience with the Word.

Reflection Questions:

- **How does putting all of those things away help us in our recovery, our faith, and our lives?**

- **What does "put away from you" mean?**

CHAPTER SEVENTY

LIFTED FROM THE ASH HEAP

P salm 113:5–7 Who is like the Lord our God, who is seated on high, who looks down on the heavens and the earth? He raises the poor from the dust and lifts the needy from the ash heap.

There should be nothing more comforting to us as recovering addicts than knowing our God and Creator, who looks down on the heavens we look up to, will help us when we fall.

Reflection Questions:

- How do we ask Him to raise us from the dust and lift us from the ash heap?

- Will He listen even if we fall often?

Chapter Seventy-One

LIGHT MY LAMP

Psalm 18:28 *For it is You who light my lamp; the Lord my God lightens my darkness.*

Dwelling in darkness can be just how we live or exist as an addict. No hope, no peace, hurting our loved ones, hurting ourselves—is an unfortunate reality of the life of an addict. Often not even seeking light but just accepting our darkness. Let the Lord light that spark that gives your hope a lamp of fire—a burning fire. Let Him illuminate that darkness you thought impenetrable. Even the thickest darkness recedes at the smallest light. Once the Lord lights your lamp, He may just use that lamp to start a fire.

Reflection Questions:
- **What does the darkness of addiction feel like?**

- **How bad has it been for you?**

- **Have you asked the Lord to light your lamp and lighten your darkness?**

Chapter Seventy-Two

LIVING FREE

Titus 2:11–12*For the grace of God has appeared, bringing salvation for all people, instructing us to turn from godless living and sinful pleasures. We are to live self-controlled, upright, and godly lives in the present age.*

The grace of God for all people, even us, even through the worst mistakes we have made. Ungodliness and worldly passions lead to unhealthy habits and misery. Living godly isn't boring and devoid of fun. It's learning to enjoy the world not chemically altered. The inner peace God brings allows us to not be restless, to think something always has to be going on, or seeking some kind of rush, however we may get it, to be happy. Stillness does not equal boredom. Quietness should not make us antsy. We embrace our connection to God, who is connected to all things, and find new things exciting, new beauty we never saw, and a stillness and quietness we embrace with our soul.

Reflection Questions

- **What does God's grace entail to you?**

- **Can you comprehend living an addiction-free life?**

CHAPTER SEVENTY-THREE

LOOK TO JESUS

Hebrews 12:2 Looking to Jesus, the founder & perfecter of our faith, who for the joy that was set before Him endured the cross, despising the shame, & is seated at the right hand of the throne of God.

We look to Jesus, the One who started it all, to be our strength, our provider, our teacher, our Savior. Saved us from things which we could not save ourselves. Despise shame as He did. Being wise & learning from mistakes is healthy, letting the shame of past mistakes keep you from making progress is not. Let He who sits at the right hand of God lead you to recovery & a new life you never thought possible.

Reflection Questions:

- **Do you look to Jesus for help?**

- **Who is He to you right now?**

- **Who would you like Him to be?**

- **Can He who sits at the right hand of God even hear you?**

CHAPTER SEVENTY-FOUR

LOVE ONE ANOTHER

John 13:34–35 **A new commandment I give to you, that you love one another: just as I have loved you, you also are to love one another. By this all people will know that you are My disciples, if you have love for one another.**

Loving others means we don't want to hurt them or cause undo stress or have them absorbing the consequences of our actions. Just as He loved us means He does not want to see us suffer either. Expunging hate, bitterness, insecurity, vengeance, and resentment from our hearts and filling it with His love makes us a whole new person. One with peace and hope.

Reflection Questions:
- **How does "love one another" play out in everyday life with the people around you?**

- **What do you need to let go of so that you can embrace love?**

CHAPTER SEVENTY-FIVE

LOVE THAT DOESN'T QUIT

1 Corinthians 13:6–7*Love does not rejoice at wrongdoing, but rejoices with the truth. Love bears all things, believes all things, hopes all things, endures all things.*

Do you get happy when you take that drink, do that line, smoke that bowl, slide that $20 into that machine, open that porn? That's not love. Not love for God, for your loved ones, or yourself. Love isn't in embracing the rush of your addiction but standing in the truth of the damage it's done and will continue to do as long as you do it. Love never gives up on recovery, never loses faith or hope, and endures through all. God's love is beyond our comprehension and never, ever gives up on us.

Reflection Questions:

- **How much love do you have for God, your loved ones, and yourself?**

- **Do you find yourself worthy of love?**

- **Does God find you worthy of love?**

- **Which matters more?**

CHAPTER SEVENTY-SIX

LOVED BY GOD

Revelation 21:4 He will wipe every tear from their eyes, and there will be no more death or sorrow or crying or pain. All these things are gone forever.

This speaks to the very nature of the Most High God who created us. Mankind fell, there's nothing we can do about our fallen nature and sinful flesh. But we were created to not experience these things by this God who loves us. The Word says He saved every tear we've cried. That's not a God of vengeance, wrath, & punishment, that is a God whose love for us is beyond our understanding. His only requirement—seek Him. If we choose to seek worldly things He lets us, and that's all we'll ever know. If we seek Him, we learn the depth of the love He has for us, as much as a person can understand divine love that is.

Reflection Questions:
- **Do you ever feel loved by God?**

- **Are you loved by God?**

- **How can we learn about God's love?**

Chapter Seventy-Seven

LOVING DISCIPLINE

Proverbs 12:1 **Whoever loves discipline loves knowledge, but he who hates reproof is stupid.**

Just by the very nature of being an addict it is evident that discipline in our lives is lacking if non-existent. We tend to hate it. No one should be telling me what to do, I'm an adult, or it's my life, don't tell me how to live. Self-discipline is a foreign concept. We indulge the desires of our flesh and how and when we see fit, even unto our own demise. One of the best parts about our faith is we don't have to learn self-discipline on our own, but are instructed to ask the Spirit to help us learn. We learn discipline makes us better, less selfish people. Reproof or correction from a friend or loved one is usually out of love or concern, and if you hate it, well...

Reflection Questions:

- **Where does discipline stand in your life?**

- **What does "loves discipline loves knowledge" mean?**

- **What are some ways you can implement discipline in your life?**

Chapter Seventy-Eight

MADE CLEAN

Acts 10:15 *And the voice came to him a second time, Do not call anything impure that God has made clean.*

Dwelling on things we've done can be a weight holding us back from moving forward. Do not call anything impure that God has made clean, including yourself. Guilt can be more than a hurdle to recovery; it can be a road to relapse. Who you are and who you were are no longer connected—even if you've just started building the new you. Once God has made you clean, you are clean, a new creation. So forget about who you used to be and walk confidently into the new you.

Reflection Questions:
- **Does guilt linger in your life?**

- **What's the difference between healthy and unhealthy guilt?**

- **How did God make you clean—or how can God make you clean?**

Chapter Seventy-Nine

MAKE TIME TO BUILD FAITH

R omans 1:17 For in it the righteousness of God is revealed from faith for faith, as it is written, "The righteous shall live by faith."

The gospel, in it the righteousness of God is revealed from people with faith in God for people to find faith in God. How do we break free from things that have held us in spiritual oppression? By connecting spiritually to the things that will set us free—the gospel of Jesus Christ. Start up with a verse or two a day if you struggle to read the Word. But commit to consistency however much it is. Non-negotiable. Ask the Spirit for help in prayer. "I'm just too busy"—but add up your phone, TV, computer screen time per day, and then ask yourself again if you don't have time. The righteous shall live by faith, not perfection. So make time to build your faith.

Reflection Questions:

- **What are the qualifications for God to find you righteous?**

- **What can you do to make reading time possible?**

- **How does reading the gospel build faith?**

CHAPTER EIGHTY

MINDFUL OF ME

*P**salm 8:3–5 When I look at Your heavens, the work of Your fingers, the moon and the stars, which You have set in place, what is man that You are mindful of him, and the son of man that You care for him? Yet You have made him a little lower than the heavenly beings and crowned him with glory and honor.*

This God that created the heavens, the moon, and the stars with His hand is mindful of you. He sees you. He hears you. He cares about you. He doesn't want to see you suffer or be in bondage. He's always there waiting to help. We pull away from Him, not Him from us. Crowned with glory and honor—not created for condemnation and shame. Reach out to this great God, a being beyond human comprehension, and find peace.

Reflection Questions

Does the God of all creation seem too big to know you and your problems?

How do we know He isn't?

What does *mindful* mean?

CHAPTER EIGHTY-ONE

MIRACLE WORKER

John 9:32 Never since the world began has it been heard that anyone opened the eyes of a man born blind.

So what problem do you have that the Lord can't help you with? What problem can we not lay at His feet? What problem is He unwilling to help us with? He is a miracle worker. He loves when His children ask Him for help with anything troubling them. Jesus made the lame walk and the blind see—He can heal any affliction, including addiction. Never forget the words Jesus said to those He healed: *"Your faith has healed you."*

Reflection Questions:

How do we tap into the miraculous healing power of the Lord?

Does He want to heal us?

CHAPTER EIGHTY-TWO

MUSTARD SEED FAITH

Matthew 17:20 He said to them, Because of your little faith. For truly I say to you, if you have faith like the grain of a mustard seed, you will say to this mountain, Move from here to there, and it will move. Nothing would be impossible.

Little faith. It's easy to lose faith when we're battered by life, living in a prison we ourselves built. It's easy to tell ourselves He doesn't hear us or we've been found unworthy. But Jesus says it only takes the faith the size of a mustard seed, one of the smallest seeds, to move mountains. There's no affliction too big or anyone too far gone that the Lord can't help. Find that seed in yourself. Plant it, water it, care for it, grow it, and nothing will be impossible for you.

Reflection Questions:

How big is your faith right now?

Have you tried to have faith but couldn't?

Can faith be grown? And if so, how?

Chapter Eighty-Three

My Redeemer Lives

J **ob 19:25 For I know that my Redeemer lives, and at the last He will stand upon the earth.**

Some scholars believe Job is the oldest book in the Bible. It is definitely one of the oldest. Yet Job knew Christ the Redeemer lived even then and would stand on earth in the end. If Job had faith in Him even before He knew His name or who He was, we can surely have faith in Him because we know who He is and the miracles He did and continues to perform every day, and the price He willingly paid for us.

Reflection Questions:

- **What does the name Redeemer mean?**

- **How does He redeem us from our lives of addiction?**

CHAPTER EIGHTY-FOUR

NEAR AND NOT FAR

Acts 17:27 *God did this so that they would seek Him and perhaps reach out for and find Him though He is not far from any of us.*

Can you imagine that the God who created the universe—who could just demand our attention—instead sits and hopes that we'll seek Him? That these beings He created would reach out and find Him. But we're so distracted by the world we don't give Him one thought, much less seek Him. The throes of addiction can be all-encompassing, leaving thought for nothing but itself.It seems so big, to seek God, but He is right there near you. Waiting for you to call on Him so He can set you free.

Reflection Questions:

- **Have you ever sought God?**

- **What were the circumstances if you have?**

- **Does the thought of God near you bother you because**

you feel filthy?

- **Why should we not feel this way?**

CHAPTER EIGHTY-FIVE

NEVER ALONE

Ecclesiastes 4:10 For if they fall, one will lift up his fellow. **But woe to him who is alone when he falls and has not another to lift him up.**

At times, as addicts, we've had friends or family pick us up after we've done something wrong, gotten too drunk and did something stupid, blew our whole check in a lotto machine, got caught looking at things we said we wouldn't, etc. They pick us up because they love us and care about us. But eventually, over time, they get tired of picking us up. It's hard to bear the burdens of one's own life and to have to constantly help someone else up who keeps falling. That's why we turn to the Lord — because we'll never fall alone again and, over time, learn to stand, not fall so much or sometimes at all. He says, "I will never leave you or forsake you. No one can snatch you from My hand."

Reflection Questions:

- **Has your addiction brought you to a place of feeling alone?**

- **How does it feel when everyone's tired of picking you up?**

- **Will the Lord ever leave you alone?**

CHAPTER EIGHTY-SIX

NEW EVERY MORNING

Lamentations 3:22–23 **The steadfast love of the Lord never ceases; His mercies never come to an end; they are new every morning; great is Your faithfulness.**

This verse says the Lord loves us without limits. There's no such thing as too great a sin or too many sins to be forgiven, because His mercies never cease. Not only does He not hold onto our sins in our distant past, He doesn't hold onto our sins from yesterday. Unceasing faithfulness to the children whom He loves, who call on His name.

Reflection Questions:

- **If His mercies are new every morning, how should we start every day?**

- **Jeremiah was a prophet and knew God personally—what do these verses tell you about God's nature and character?**

CHAPTER EIGHTY-SEVEN

NO CONDEMNATION

Romans 8:1 There is therefore now no condemnation for those who are in Christ Jesus.

Condemnation from the world or other people can hurt, but self-condemnation can hinder and sometimes completely sabotage our walk in recovery. We can take great joy in the fact that there is no condemnation to us who call Jesus Christ our Lord and Savior. Mistakes and backsliding are a part of our humanity. But not considering ourselves broken or unworthy because of our mistakes is vital to our recovery. Stay repentant and move forward. Progress is attainable every day; perfection is not.

Reflection Questions:

- How can we as sinners, living sinful lives, have no condemnation despite the things we've done?

- How do we let go of self-condemnation?

- What does "in Christ Jesus" mean?

CHAPTER EIGHTY-EIGHT

NOTHING TOO HARD FOR GOD

Jeremiah 32:26–27 **Then the word of the LORD came to Jeremiah: Behold, I am the God of all flesh. Is anything too hard for Me?**

It is so easy when we are in the midst of overwhelming struggles or just the struggles of everyday life to forget that we see our problems as they feel to us. Huge, insurmountable, overwhelming problems too big for us to see past them. The good news is we don't have to. This verse God is literally saying, What can't I do? What problem is too big for He who created all life? We can sit in self-pity, worried & depressed or we can ask the Almighty for help & let Him do what He does—help His children who love Him when they call on Him. Exercise that free will He gave you to ask Him for help.

Reflection Questions:

- **Are your problems overwhelming at times?**

- **When they are does it lead to indulging your addictions?**

- **Have you asked God for help?**

Chapter Eighty-Nine

ONLY ONE NAME

A cts 4:12 And there is salvation in no one else, for there is no other name under heaven given among men by which we must be saved.

Jesus Christ, the only name by which we are saved. King of kings and Lord of lords. The one who loved you so much that He died a terrible death so you could be free. Not a judgmental dictator waiting to punish you for every mistake, but one who has grace and mercy beyond what we deserve, loving us no matter what. Eternal salvation is what He gives, but sometimes we have to start with salvation from ourselves and our addictions. Ask Him for help. Tell Him you can't do it without Him. Watch Him help you find peace.

Reflection Questions:

- **Have you called on Jesus' name to help you in recovery?**

- **If not, why?**

- **Do you believe He loves you?**

CHAPTER NINETY

OPEN THE DOOR

Luke 11:9 *And I tell you, ask, and it will be given to you; seek, and you will find; knock, and it will be opened to you.*

How do you know what the Lord can help you with if you've never asked? How can you know Him or who He is if you've never sought Him? Asking Him to get you out of or keep you from going to jail doesn't count. So many have never even tried, yet somehow know He doesn't exist or isn't willing to help them. Knock, with an open heart and an open mind, and watch Him open the door to a new life.

Reflection Questions

- **Have you ever asked God for help outside of getting you out of a bad situation?**

- **How can you seek Him?**

- **What is the overall point of this verse?**

CHAPTER NINETY-ONE

PEACE BEYOND THE WORLD

John 14:27 Peace I leave with you; My peace I give you. Not as the world gives do I give to you. Let not your hearts be troubled, neither let them be afraid.

Peace... elusive, fleeting peace. Fleeting for most people, almost unheard of in the life of an addict. But Jesus gives us His peace. An every day, unshakable peace. Not a worldly peace that comes & goes but a divine peace that those that know Him show. Ups & downs, highs & lows, a peace inside that says: You got this, because I am with you. Addicts know all too well what a troubled heart is and what it's like to be afraid. Seek Him and know what it's like to have peace in the depths of your soul.

Reflection Questions:
- **How does your addiction disrupt your peace?**

- Have you ever sought peace before?

- What does "Not as the world gives do I give to you" mean?

CHAPTER NINETY-TWO

PERFECT IN WEAKNESS

2 **Corinthians 12:9 But He said to me, My grace is sufficient for you, for My power is made perfect in weakness. Therefore, I will boast all the more gladly of my weaknesses, so that the power of Christ may rest upon me.**

This is the heart of the philosophy of our recovery group. His grace gives us what we need to succeed. It supplies what we are missing. There's no shame in saying I cannot be who I'm supposed to be without Him. It's the very purpose for which we were created, to fellowship with God for His glory. His power completes us.

Reflection Questions:

- **How do we receive God's grace?**

- **Why would we boast in our weaknesses?**

- **How is His power made perfect in our weakness?**

Chapter Ninety-Three

PRAY FOR EACH OTHER

James 5:16 Therefore, confess your sins to one another & pray for one another, that you may be healed. The prayer of a righteous person has great power as it is working.

Confessing our sins to one another can lift burdens we carry of guilt for pain we've caused, damage we've done. Pray for each other. As believers we depend on each other to be prayer warriors, but don't just receive, pray for others as well. Praying for others can help them but also helps us. It helps to know you're helping even while you're struggling. There is no greater help you have available than asking the Lord to help someone. And yes, if Jesus is your Lord & Savior you are righteous by His sacrifice. So pray for others & yourself. Make it a habit & watch it work.

Reflection Questions:
- **Have you ever confessed to anyone? Why or why not?**

- **How often do you pray?**

- **What is prayer to you?**

Chapter Ninety-Four

PRAYER AND PEACE

Philippians 4:6–7 **Do not be anxious about anything, but in everything, by prayer and petition, with thanksgiving, present your requests to God. And the peace of God, which transcends all understanding, will guard your hearts and your minds in Christ Jesus.**

When in doubt—pray. When tempted—pray. When anxious—pray. When depressed—pray. When happy and thankful—pray. Prayer is a necessity. Every circumstance in life, bad or good. There's no thanks too big or problem too small—just pray. The Lord created us to be connected with Him, and prayer is that connection.

Reflection Questions:

- **What can give us anxiety bad enough to lead to relapse?**

- **Prayer and petition with thanksgiving—present your requests to God—how does that work?**

CHAPTER NINETY-FIVE

PREPARE YOUR MIND

1 **Peter 1:13 Therefore, prepare your minds for action; be self-controlled; set your hope fully on the grace to be given to you when Christ Jesus is revealed.**

Just like anything else in life, a mind set on recovery and self-control takes practice and training. Even long-time believers can have bad habits, negative thought processes, or cycles and routines of sin and relapse ingrained in them as habit. Taking thoughts captive and re-training our minds takes consistent effort and practice.

Reflection Questions:
- **How do we prepare our minds?**

- **How important is self-control?**

- **Why do we set our hope fully on the grace to be given?**

CHAPTER NINETY-SIX

PRESERVED SPIRIT

J   **ob 10:12 You have granted me life and steadfast love, and your care has preserved my spirit.**

God created us and loves us. We are not just ants that He watches, not caring, hoping that we stumble upon Him. He created us to know Him, to fellowship with and glorify Him. When we reach out to Him, He preserves our spirit and spiritual health. Through God, we can be led to overall health as a human being. We are not ants on a rock hurling through space. We are the masterpiece of God's creation, loved by Him before we were born.

Reflection Questions:

- **As an addict, have you questioned your own existence?**

- **What came with the life in which you were created?**

- **Is our spirit ever too far gone for God to preserve it?**

Chapter Ninety-Seven

PRICELESS LOVE

Psalm 36:7 **How precious is your steadfast love, O God! The children of mankind take refuge in the shadow of your wings.**

How precious is God's steadfast love? It's priceless. It's the most valuable thing any person has in their lifetime. The love of God gives you peace of mind, peace of heart and soul, and the strength to endure the hardships of life without falling apart.

We find refuge under His wings because He is our protector, our parent—just as we are to our children, but perfect and unfailing. So don't trade God's love for your love of worldly things. This love is the only thing we ever have in this life that is truly priceless.

Reflection Questions:
- **How precious is God's love to you?**

- **What does steadfast mean?**

- **Do you need refuge at times?**

- **Where can you find it?**

Chapter Ninety-Eight

REJOICING IN SUFFERING

Romans 5:3–5 Not only that, but we rejoice in our sufferings, knowing that suffering produces endurance, and endurance produces character, and character produces hope, and hope does not put us to shame, because God's love has been poured into our hearts through the Holy Spirit who has been given to us.

God says He uses everything to work for our own good. Suffering also produces good things in our lives. Don't take suffering as punishment—God uses it as enrichment. God uses it to transform us into better people. Suffering isn't condemnation from God, it's refinement through fire.

Reflection Questions:

- **What are some other things suffering can produce for us? (Wisdom, knowledge, strength, gratitude)**

- **What does "hope does not put us to shame" mean?**

- **What are some examples in your life of suffering producing something positive?**

CHAPTER NINETY-NINE

REDEEMED LIFE

Lamentations 3:57–58 You came when I called on You; You said, 'Do not fear! You have taken up my cause, O Lord; You have redeemed my life.

If you call on Him, He will come! For some reason, this first step seems simple but can be a sticking point for many. The act of submitting can be scary. Fear of unworthiness, doubt, or what it means to call on Him. Do not fear! If you call on Him, He comes in love, not judgment, to heal, not to condemn. He will take up your cause with you and redeem your life from hopelessness and addiction's constant toxic cycle. Call on the Lord. He loves you.

Reflection Questions:

- **Have you ever called on the Lord with a sincere heart?**

- **If not, what has held you back?**

- **What is scarier — calling on the Lord or where your life will go if you don't?**

RENEWED MIND

Romans 12:2 **Do not be conformed to this world, but be transformed by the renewal of your mind, that by testing you may discern what is the will of God, what is good and acceptable and perfect.**

The world will tell you that drinking, drugs, porn, gambling, etc., are all normal and everyone does them—no big deal. When you accept Christ into your life, it renews your mind, and the very way you see the world and what aligns with God's Word begins to change. It's not about seeing what you're doing as right in your own eyes or not, because God wants what's best for us. He's not a dictator imposing rules on us. He's a loving God who wants what's best for us and knows what that is better than we do, because He created us.

Reflection Questions:

- **When you look at the world today, is it something you want to be conformed to?**

- **How does renewal of our minds transform us?**

- **Why is discernment so important?**

RESCUED FROM THE PIT

Psalm 30:2–3 O Lord my God, I cried to you for help, and you have healed me. O Lord, you have brought up my soul from Sheol; you restored me to life from among those who go down to the pit.

In the depths of despair and hopelessness, call out to the Lord. He is waiting, ready to heal. We can experience resurrection in the midst of life. Addiction can make us like the walking dead. Dead to the world around us. We can be saved, from addiction, from ourselves. We need only call on Him and let Him resurrect us as a new creation. One with hope and the knowledge that the Living God loves us.

Reflection Questions:

- **What stops us from crying out to the Lord?**

- **What is the pit from which we ask to be saved?**

RIGHTEOUS GAINS

Proverbs 16:8 *Better is a little with righteousness than great gains with injustice.*

Financial troubles are burdensome. Very few people do not experience them, and the pressure they lay on us can be a very real part of our addictions. Only there are very few addictions that don't multiply the burdens. The addictions themselves can lead us to doing things we wouldn't normally do to get them. An addiction put in check is almost always more money in our pocket. Money gained unjustly always has consequences tied to it. You may struggle financially but give thanks for what you do have. Work more, work hard, try for promotions or jobs that pay better. Do things the right way, and be thankful for what you have.

Reflection Questions:
- **Do finances cause stress in your life?**

- **To the point it leads to using sometimes?**

- If you added up what you spend on your addiction per month, how much is it?

- What could you do with that extra money?

CHAPTER ONE HUNDRED THREE

SANCTIFIED IN TRUTH

John 17:16–17 *They are not of the world, just as I am not of the world. Sanctify them in truth; Your Word is truth.*

We are not of the world. We belong to God, but we let worldly things and worldly passions lead us away from Him. The truth is, you were not meant to live in bondage to any worldly thing. The truth is that God loves you and wants you to know Him. So open your Bible and learn how much God loves you. Jesus Christ is the truth, and who He sets free is free indeed. The hopeless find hope, the restless find stillness, the tormented find peace, those in bondage find freedom, and those dead inside are brought back to life.

Reflection Questions
- **What does "not of the world" mean?**

- **What does it mean to be sanctified in truth?**

- **Is truth objective or subjective?**

Search My Heart

P salm 139:23–24 Search me, O God, & know my heart! Try me & know my thoughts! And see if there be any grievous way in me, & lead me in the way everlasting!

Appearances can fool people for a time. You look fine but inside you are anything but fine. Ask God to look inside of you. Ask Him to change your heart, your mind, your spirit. He can see things inside of us that we can't & He knows how they work better than we do. Ask Him to help with your urge for your addiction, anxiety, depression, anger, envy, & everything that troubles you & hinders your recovery. Ask Him to make the changes you need for recovery, & watch hope & peace take over your life.

Reflection Questions:

- **Do you have things in you you don't want God to see?**

- **Does He know your thoughts anyway?**

- **So why have to ask?**

CHAPTER ONE HUNDRED FIVE
SEEK WISDOM

I saiah 5:21 Woe to those who are wise in their own eyes and shrewd in their own sight.

An inability to seek wisdom outside ourselves is a pit many of us fall into. Thinking, "I'm not perfect, but I know what's best for me. I know what I can handle." An inability to think a different way and be honest with ourselves is part of why we continue to make bad choices and sabotage our own lives. "I can handle just one" of anything to any addict is a self-issued ticket to misery and continued bondage. Man-made wisdom destroys; divine wisdom gives life and sets free.

Reflection Questions:

- **Do you have the ability to be completely honest with yourself about where your choices and addiction have led you?**

- **What is wisdom?**

- **Does pride get in the way of asking for wisdom?**

- **Why is it so hard to acknowledge that we lack wisdom?**

SENSE AND SOUL

Proverbs 19:8 *Whoever gets sense loves his own soul; he who keeps understanding will discover good.*

Whoever gets sense? It means the sense to know when something isn't good for you. To us addicts, the sense to know that something is destroying our lives and hurting the ones we love. The sense to know that there is a better way to live. Then we keep this understanding and act on it. We understand that we have to change, and that it has to be today, not tomorrow. In an addict's life, we do a whole lot of things that don't make any sense. But when we understand this and change, we discover good—we discover God.

Reflection Questions:

- **Has addiction led you to do senseless things?**

- **What does it mean to love your own soul?**

- **Why is it they who "keep" understanding discover good?**

SENT AHEAD

Genesis 45:5 **And now do not be angry or distressed with yourselves for selling me to this place. It was God who sent me here ahead of you to preserve your lives.**

Joseph's brothers sold him as a slave because of their jealousy, but Joseph did not hate them because he knew God had sent him there for a purpose. Joseph had not wronged anyone, yet he was made a slave. Joseph hadn't committed any crimes, yet he was imprisoned—yet he held no grudge and sought no revenge. He knew, as we do, that hard circumstances aren't always punishment or due to the unfairness of life. Sometimes they are a part of God's plan, maybe even His plan to save our lives. No human being is given a life without hardships. Don't be resentful or bitter or revengeful. Praise God through them.

Reflection Questions:

- Do you praise God when things are good and question Him when they're bad?

- What can we do to keep our faith even through suffering?

Sheep of His Pasture

Psalm 100:3 Know that the Lord, He is God! It is He who made us, and we are His; we are His people, and the sheep of His pasture.

The Lord our God is our Creator. We belong to Him, not to the world. He is our Shepherd and we are His sheep. Always there, always watching. We are never alone. Sometimes the darkness of addiction is lonely and isolating, but our Shepherd is there with us in our darkest times and worst moments. Call on His name when you feel alone or feel like you're failing.

Reflection Questions:
- **What does "we are His" mean to you?**

- **What does a shepherd do for the sheep of His pasture?**

SHEEP WITHOUT A SHEPHERD

M **ark 6:34 When He went ashore He saw a great crowd, and He had compassion on them, because they were like sheep without a shepherd. So He began teaching them many things.**

Sheep without a shepherd. Aren't we all before we find Christ? Buried in addiction, troubles, and distractions. Always finding an excuse to continue doing what we're doing regardless of the consequences or who it's hurting. The Good Shepherd leaves the 99 to find the one lost sheep. He cares for, loves, protects, and teaches His sheep. Let Him teach you how to be free and have hope.

Reflection Questions:
- **Are you worthy of Jesus' compassion?**

- **What do shepherds do?**

- **What are some of the things you can learn from Jesus?**

CHAPTER ONE HUNDRED TEN

SHIELD AND ROCK

2 Samuel 22:31–32 This God—His way is perfect; the word of the Lord proves true; He is a shield for all those who take refuge in Him. For who is God, but the Lord? And who is a rock, except our God?

Our God is a God who we can trust no matter what. He is perfect, and His love for us is perfect. His words are always true, and we should not take struggles to mean that He does not see us or finds us unworthy of His protection because of our imperfections. Even the most godly people in the Bible faced trials and temptations. It didn't take away from who they were with Him—it was where their relationship with Him was forged.

Reflection Questions:

- **How do we take refuge in the Lord?**

- **Why do we sometimes doubt God or His protection?**

- **What does it mean that God is our shield and our rock?**

- **What is the evidence that God's Word proves true?**

CHAPTER ONE HUNDRED ELEVEN

SOVEREIGN PURPOSE

Isaiah 14:24 The LORD of hosts has sworn: "As I have planned, so it shall be, and as I have purposed, so it shall stand."

The LORD never planned for us to be mired in addiction. His purpose for us isn't suffering and living in chains. His will is sovereign and absolute. Tap in to the power of the One who cannot be denied, no matter who or what comes against Him. We empower ourselves by submitting to Him. There is no higher power, no voice louder, no throne higher than the LORD our God.

Reflection Questions:

- **How do we find out what God's plan and purpose for our lives are?**

- **What's the one thing that can interfere with His plan and purpose for our lives?**

CHAPTER ONE HUNDRED TWELVE

SPIRIT OF POWER

2 Timothy 1:7 For the Spirit God gave us does not make us timid, but gives us power, love and self-discipline.

When we embark on the journey of recovery with the Lord, a certain boldness must be claimed. Not of ourselves, but in the knowledge that the Lord stands with us. That it is not our flesh fighting our addiction but the power of the Spirit of God. We stand in love—the love we are assured God has for us—and the very important process we sometimes face of learning to love ourselves. Through Christ's Spirit of love and power we learn to not only have self-discipline to stop the action of giving in to our addiction, but the ability to take thoughts captive and extinguish them before they have a chance to lead us to fall.

Reflection Questions
- **What is the Spirit God gave us?**

- **How do we tap into the Spirit's power?**

STEADFAST UNDER TRIAL

James 1:12 Blessed is the man who remains steadfast under trial, for when he has stood the test, he will receive the crown of life, which God has promised to those who love Him.

We're always under trial, that's life. Sometimes big, sometimes small, but 100% peace is rare in the world we live in. Worldly peace is anyway. Divine peace comes from God, and gives us joy in the midst of trials. Joy in knowing that life can be hard but God is always with us. It can be so hard that we question sometimes — why? why me? why now? I'm exhausted and spent. Don't numb yourself or seek a temporary fix in these times, call on God, read His Word, know He loves you. There's people that have suffered horrifically and still kept the faith. Love your Creator, cling to His promise, reject worldly relief which just makes things worse.

Reflection Questions:

- **How do we build steadfastness in ourselves?**

- **Does standing the test mean being perfect?**

- **Can we feel the effects of the crown of life in this life?**

STRENGTH
FOR THE RACE

Jeremiah 12:5 **If you have raced with men and they have tired you out, how will you compete with horses? If you stumble and fall on open ground, what will you do in the thickets near the Jordan?**

Basically, this is saying — if you can't endure the small challenges in life, how can you endure the big ones? If a bad day at work makes you relapse, how will you handle a loved one passing away? Our spiritual life is no different than our physical life — it must be exercised and made strong. Ready yourself for the inevitable big tests by making yourself strong through the everyday tests. We will stumble. How hard and how often is the question.

Reflection Questions:

- **Have you ever overblown a small problem as an excuse to indulge your addiction?**

- **Have you tried to strengthen your spirit?**

- **How do we do that?**

CHAPTER ONE HUNDRED FIFTEEN

TAKE HEART

John 16:33 I have said these things to you, that in me you may have peace. In the world you will have tribulation. But take heart; I have overcome the world.

The words of Jesus throughout the gospel are to give us the peace of knowing a reality and destiny beyond the world that often defies us. The peace of knowing the Son of God loved each and every one of us so much that He suffered a horrific death for us willingly and gladly. Whatever troubles and trials this world puts before us every day, our Lord and Savior Jesus Christ has overcome them all. Overwhelming problems to us are nothing to Him. We lean on Him in all circumstances, good or bad.

Reflection Questions:

- **What is the relationship between peace and recovery?**

- **"I have overcome the world"—how can that help us through tribulation?**

CHAPTER ONE HUNDRED SIXTEEN

TAKE REFUGE

*P**salm 34:22* **The LORD redeems the life of His servants; none who take refuge in Him will be condemned.**

The Lord redeems us. Out of addiction, out of spiritual bankruptcy, out of death itself. To redeem means to compensate for, to atone, to make amends for, or to save from. It also means to regain possession of. We gave ourselves to addiction, but if we cry out to Him, He gladly reclaims us as His own.

If, God forbid, you relapse, continue to call out—take refuge in Him. Your mind and the enemy will tell you, *look what you did! He doesn't want you anymore,* all lies. Continue to take refuge in Him—**NO MATTER** WHAT. You'll never be perfect, but always take refuge in Him. He will redeem your life.

Reflection Questions:

- **Who are His servants?**

- **Are they also His children?**

- **Which people who take refuge in Him will be con-**

demned?

Chapter One Hundred Seventeen

TESTIFIED FOR

J ob 16:19–21 Even now, behold, my witness is in heaven, and He who testifies for me is on high. My friends scorn me; my eye pours out tears to God, that He would argue the case of a man with God, as a son of man does with his neighbor.

Even Job knew he had a witness in heaven testifying for him. He just didn't know Him by name as we do—Jesus Christ. Many reasons our friends scorned us while in addiction's chains, but Jesus never did. He wishes we never had to be brought so low by the weight of addiction that we come to Him crawling and weeping—but if that's the case, He still welcomes us with open arms. We don't have to be at that point to make that choice either—if we recognize something is leading us somewhere we don't want to be and seek a better way. The Way, the Truth, and the Life—Jesus Christ.

Reflection Questions:

- **At the worst of our worst, does Jesus ever scorn us?**

- **Does God care about the tears we've cried if they're of our own doing?**

- **How does Jesus testify and argue our case before God?**

CHAPTER ONE HUNDRED EIGHTEEN

THE ONLY NAME THAT SAVES

Acts 4:12 And there is salvation in no one else, for there is no other name under heaven given among men by which we must be saved.

Jesus Christ, the only name by which we are saved. King of kings, Lord of lords. The one who loved you so much that He died a terrible death so you could be free. Not a judgmental dictator waiting to punish you for every mistake, but one who has grace & mercy beyond what we deserve, loving us no matter what. Eternal salvation is what He gives, but sometimes we have to start with salvation from ourselves & our addictions. Ask Him for help. Tell Him you can't do it without Him. Watch Him help you find peace.

Reflection Questions:

- **Have you called on Jesus' name to help you in recovery?**

- **If not, why?**

- **Do you believe He loves you?**

THIRST FOR
THE LORD

P salm 143:6 I stretch out **my hands to You; my soul thirsts
for You like a parched land. Selah.**

Yearning for the Lord. Stretching our hands out to Him because we
want to know Him so badly. Bringing ourselves to a place where we
thirst for the Lord instead of thirsting for the very things destroying
our lives. When you come to the place where you thirst for the Lord
more than anything, you won't be perfect or sinless, but you will have
a realization of what true hope, joy, and peace are. Peace of mind, peace
of spirit, peace in your life—not dictated by circumstances.

Reflection Questions:

- **What does the phrase "I stretch out my hands to You"
  symbolize?**

- **If your soul thirsts for the Lord, what will He do for
  you?**

Chapter One Hundred Twenty

TOO HEAVY TO CARRY

Psalm 38:4 **For my iniquities have gone over my head; like a heavy burden, they are too heavy for me.**

Man, the weight of our wrongs while addiction ruled our lives can be *heavy*. People hurt, relationships damaged, jobs lost, bills unpaid, betrayals we've committed. The realization of the damage we've caused is a heavy burden to bear.

So heavy, they weigh down progress and improvement. What's the best way to mend fences? To change. To get better and do better, starting *now*. You can't erase the past, but you can focus on building a better future. You can't delete old memories, but when you're creating new good ones, those old ones are much harder to remember.

Reflection Questions:

- **Are your wrongdoings in addiction overwhelming?**

- **Do they keep you from moving forward?**

- **Who forgives iniquities and lifts burdens?**

TO THE GOD WHO SEES ME

I tremble at Your might, Knowing I'm a sinful man— But You've never given me reason to fear, You made me part of Your plan.

I seek to understand You, But my mind is overwhelmed. Your being cannot be understood By this lowly human shell.

I love You like I've never loved, You are my purpose seen. Though I can't love like You have loved From before the earth had been—

Still I love You with all my heart And everything I am. For when I was dead, You raised me up— This beaten, broken man.

How can the God who created all, Who measured the heavens with His hand, Take this broken, beaten man And make him able to stand?

You took a shattered shell of clay, And pieced it back to whole. Then snatched me from the enemy— "That's My sheep that you have stole."

You say You loved me long before You knit me in the womb. Then, like Brother Lazarus, Said, "Come out of that tomb."

I heard Your voice and came awake, And stepped into the light. There my Lord did wait for me, And held me to Him tight.

If I start today and thank You Straight through a thousand lives, It would not yet be enough—Yet this man strives

To let my Lord and Savior know None can rise above The Lord and God who gave me life— Forever I will love.

A FINAL WORD FROM THE AUTHOR

This devotional was not written by a theologian, a scholar, or a perfect man. It was written by someone redeemed. Someone who knows what it's like to be lost, addicted, angry, afraid—and then found by grace.

If these pages reached you, encouraged you, or reminded you that you're not beyond the reach of God, then the mission was accomplished.

I go by *Servant of Truth*, because that's all I ever want to be.

Keep the focus on the One who saves, not the one He saved.

To Him be the glory.

For questions on anything from devotional entries to recovery questions contact me at servantoftruth888@gmail.com, I'll do my best to respond to each one depending on volume.

www.ingramcontent.com/pod-product-compliance
Lightning Source LLC
Chambersburg PA
CBHW060155130626
46556CB00006B/2650